Orange

Sherbet

And

Hot Chocolate

Poetry by
Richard Gordon

This book is dedicated to friends.

1979

Special thanks to my best friend and wife, Carol, who has taught me that a true friend is willing to take risk for you, and will glory in your growth. Thanks is also given to Barbara Shirley and her university Women's Club, who first "got on my case" about not being published; and to John Fletcher, a 13 year old youngster, who at summer camp read my poems and told me they made him feel "all warm inside"; and to Sybil Winston who gave me courage, by sharing her artistry. Thanks to my many friends who backed up their faith in me with financial support to complete the project. A special thanks for the Love in the world and to God who provides it.

2005

This book continues to be dedicated to friends. Carol is even more of an inspiration than twenty-five years ago when this book was first published. A special thanks to my sister Marilyn, who for more than ten years has been after me to "please make the book available again." And to my children who have made the joy reflected in their yesteryears so gratifying.

2013

To my everlasting inspiration, Carol.

ACKNOWLEDGMENTS

Poems appearing on pages 70 and 71 by Jeanette Dilg

Poem on page 47 by Monica Gordon at 16 years old

Drawing on page 101 by Carol Austin Gordon

CONTENTS

MAMA AND DADDY

SHADES OF PAIN

LUCKY ME

MY MUSE

DEAR FRIENDS

TWO BY JEANETTE

IN LOVE AGAIN

DREAMS AND WISHES

MAMA AND DADDY

Character Line

Mama,
did I see you
looking in the
mirror, stroking
a line no one else could see?
I'm saddened to know
I may have caused you
conniptions and an un-
wanted line or two.

Like when I was gathering
goose-bumps and tennis
balls, and fell from the roof?
You came a-running, wild-eyed and
with an "I-could-just-
kill-you " look on you face

But you softened, and
the lines on your brow
vanished as you cradled
my damaged arm in yours,
and with a flair of in-
difference, wiped the
dust from your eye that
I could have sworn was
a tear.

But Mama,
of all the character
I've seen on your face,
I want to believe I
brought about those
really deep lines that
suddenly appear when
you smile.

But I don't think they're
the ones I caused, be-
cause I seem to remember
those being there the
first time I fell
asleep in your arms.

DADDY

When did you first know
        you were somebody?
When did your heart
        get so big?
When did you first
        love Mom?
When did you first
        love me?

Sometimes you were
so big and strong and
scary... especially when I
had done something to dis-
please you, like steal ccandy
from the store or get tangled
in a lie. But when I needed
a champion... when I told Homer:
"My dad can whip your dad any day,"
it sure was handy that you
were so big and so
strong and so
scary.

(con't)

When I was
small I had
to walk double and
still couldn't match
your stride, but you
would always wait, take
my hand and lead me
safely through the
dark. And sometimes,
even now, I place
my trembling hand
in yours and walk
with your bigness
through an
unknown.

Daddy,
next to you
loving Mama,
you being there,
being close, was
the most precious
memory you planted
in me. Your dream
that I would someday
expand our heritage,
has given me a
Knowing of who
I am, and a need
to share your
Dream.

Daddy?
When did you first know
You were somebody?
When did your heart
Get so big?
When did you first
Love Mom?
When did you first
Love me?

I bet...
I bet it was way back when...
When your Dad
First took you
Through the dark.

SHADES OF PAIN

BLINDNESS

Blindness,
I imagine is not
so much what I feel
when I close my eyes
and walk with my hands,
but closer to the dis-
connection I felt when
I had a heart full of
love and no
takers.

CROSSED SHADOWS

For a walking moment,
      our shadows mingled
            on the beaten road . . .

But our eyes,
      riveted to our feet,
            nipped the touching there.

ROCK HARD

Looking out the window

waiting a sign from you...

Eyes red brick now

feet cold stone.

The more I wait,

The harder I get,

The less I feel.

NEW FRIENDS

A hermit and a hermit
    challenged the night
        from opposite
            directions.

Time,
    the bitter cold,
        and a clump of comfort,
    introduced the mangled souls.

            Warmed
            by the fire
        in the other's eyes,
    they parted in silence,
        old friends.

REFUGE

When I sit alone
        among the empty eyes
            of wooden smiles,
And feel the absence
        of feeling in the
            touch of friends. . .

I run to my hobbyhorse
        and ride, ride, ride
            into the sunset.

THE HURTIN'

I cannot ignore you...
I cannot dismiss your presence...
I cannot... not love you.

Every time I see you now,
    I get that uncommitted
      half-smile that rips me
        to the heart.

A word from you
    before I speak
      would soothe the pain I feel...
But all I hear from you
    is the silence
      of the hurt I caused.

I look to see inside your eyes,
    to see inside your heart,
  But your eyes
    are cased in frozen tears
      that holds my guilt within.

I CRIED LOVE

I cried the tears that wouldn't come.
I paced our hollow home and cried.
I cried your name,
    and it echoed from room to room,
    and came booming back alone.

I cried the tears that wouldn't come.
In a quiet house
    full of noisy yesterdays,
        I saw the kids that brought such joy...
But they vanished as their laughter
    washed the smile away.

I cried the tears that wouldn't come.

And in the space that was our room,
    I stroked your hair and
          kissed your lips.
I whispered to your presence:
    Come back...
    Come back my love, for
I have cried the tears that wouldn't come.

I CALLED HER MOM ONCE

Just give me the
chair, you know. I'm
tired of her heavy on
my mind. Just give
me the chair.

She took me in,
gave me chicken soup and
cornbread, and likened me
to the young warrior pictured
on the mantle. She
called me son, and I called
her Mom... once.

> *Be strong son. Be strong.*
> *You don't need that stuff*
> *no more. You got a mom now,*
> *and I got a new son. I'll*
> *keep you safe, son... keep*
> *you warm... keep you good. I'll*
> *help you be strong, son.*

It scares me bad when I'm
the animal... when I need the
stuff she hid so well to keep
me good. I wasn't me

no more. Like a Mister
Hyde, you know... 'cept it
was what I couldn't find
that made me ugly.

>   *Where's my shit, lady?*
>   *Where's my shit!*

Three minutes, or three
hours after she lay unmoving
and cold, I found my Will
taped to the back of a dead
warrior... and he gave me
comfort.

And the animal mellowed into
a little boy who cried at
the loss of cornbread and
chicken soup.

>   *Mom, please don't ever mess*
>   *with my shit.*

I'm tired of her heavy on
my mind. Just give me the
chair, you know.

HAPPY DUST

Somewhere between
    hope grown painful
      and no hope at all...

His dreams
    were ground to dust
    and snifffed
      for a fast,
        cheap ride
    to oblivion.

BREACHED LIFE

Squeezed
out the
wrong way:
Empty-eyed,
and shrivel-
spirited-young-men
fall back-
wards through
        hope,
shooting the
rust of
unrequited
   Dreams.

THE
OPULENT TENTH

As half-fed creatures
stumble beneath my dreams,
I slam shut my mind
and wrap flabby lips round
     thin hors d'oeuvres,
and smack my chops
     on mutton cheeks.

BREAK STRING BREAK

Hotel resident thirteen years,
    Forgotten,
      Alone,
And waiting to die...

Waiting through dead life
    That dreads life to end.

Hold on, hold on
      to the knotted thread...
      Tie it again,
        Tie it again--
One more day...
    Dead.

LUCKY ME

LUCKY ME

I see me,
   and I think of
     You loving me,
And I laugh
     how lucky I am
to be in love with you.

THE WAY OF LOVE

Sometimes,
When I feel the love in your eyes
I just wanna hold you
and squeeze you
right into my being.

But I kiss you
Love you, and let you be
        'cause
that'she way of love.

Sometimes,
When I see your laughing smile
I just wanna take it, clutch it,
and keep the joy of it
for sad times.

But I just smile back
and let it laugh,
        'cause
that's the way of love.

And sometimes
When we've made a beautiful moment,
I wanna stop time and live that moment
endlessly with you.

But time moves on to a memory
and a new moment,
        'cause
that's the way of love.

A TREE CALLED CAROL

I'll take a lock
of your hair,
tangle it in the
roots of a seedling
      Oak,
and watch it grow
like our kids and
      Love.

ONE JOURNEY
OF YOUR SMILE

You braid
your smile
into the hair
of laughing girls
who kiss back
the warmth into
your fingertips
that caress
my lips
whispering,
    Smile.

YOU'RE THE BLAME

Now, girl
how you feel 'bout all
this time I spend thinking 'bout you?

No need gettin' uppity and
Squintin' those eyes...
It ain't my fault,
it's yours

You're the one causing
   all the commotion
      Making me shy as a lovesick school boy
                      on one hand,
     and lettin' me know I can naturally fly
                      on the other.

It's not my fault
   you're so damn exciting...

        (That's it, Honey...
        Go on...
          Open wide
            them big brown
            beautiful
            Eyes...

          That's it...
               Smile...)

I MISS YOU

It's a kick
to be able to write and
every five minutes or so,
get up, go into our room
and kiss you gently
on the cheek
as you sleep,
waiting to make me
smile.

I miss you
as you step out to grow;
as you do your own thing...
create a space of your own,
and
   become as much
      as you command.
I love it!

   But still,
   I get up every
   five minutes
   or so, walk to
   where you'll be
   any minute now...
      (Any minute!)
   and stand there
   waiting silly
   for you
   to make me
   smile.

COMPLEMENTARY

Last night
I felt you
worry for me.
       Well,
don't worry
'bout me love,
I'm fine.
You
make me
constant and
solid.
You're the
anchor that keeps
me strong enough
to be your
Harbor.

YOU STILL EXCITE ME LIKE
THAT OLD MOON-JUNE LOVE

My heart still runs like a buzz-saw
    every time my thoughts caress the
        soft love, love-stuff, you.
My innards still get tangled
    every time I see your sassy smile.
        And every smile I con from you,
          I easily bend to naughty.
My hands still fumble
    every time they try to sneak an
        accidental touch of you.
And even still, moments after you've gone,
    my feet swim in hot-air,
        Trying,
          Trying to follow...
    Coming down,
        Only with a summer snow.
So now, my whole self goes electric
    every time
        you buzz my heart,
          tangle my innards,
            or fumble my hands
In the perennial summer of your presence.

YOU TOUCHED ME

You simply
touched my face,
and I hoped the
message that sang
through my body
was really
there.

MY MUSE

RUSTING

Waiting for

inspiration

is like

waiting for

death.

MY MUSE

Sometimes,
(only sometimes)
I have to stand up to write
'Cause the images come leaping
out of my fingertips like Nijinsky,
parading and pirouetting
across the stage fright pages
before I've had a chance to
think them.

> And I never
>   think like that!

A FIXED RACE

Give me a

headstart

with my pen,

before my

beautiful

thoughts and

perfect sayings

"jump-the-gun,"

never giving

me a chance

to catch up.

(by Monica Lynn Gordon)

FRESH FRUIT

I'm not a poet
in the classical sense.
I don't strive
to dazzle with
words or to
mystify with
symbols. I just
share my feelings.
I want to hand
them to you whole,
fresh, and fuzzy,
  Like a table setting
    of tree ripened
      fruit.

RHYME AND REASON

We string our moments
    on a web of rhyme,
as the Poet paints sounds
    on a page of time.
Life lovely echoes
    unfinished poems
completed by death.

I GOTTA SING IT TO YOU

But
I ain't no singer...
    can't carry a tune,
        never could.
I mean I invent rhythms,
notes, and octaves you ain't
never heard before. But, Love,
I got this guitar in my hand and
a song ringing in my head that
I can't carry around no more. So,
I'm unloading it right here and
now I gotta sing it to you.

DEAR FRIENDS

.

ROSCOE
LEE
BROWNE

When Roscoe

reads to us,

he takes the

twinkle from

his eyes, folds

it in his

voice, and

excites our

imaginations

with interwoven

gleams of

fright,

warmth, and

delight.

MAHALIA IS GONE

Mahalia is gone.

Mahalia is gone and I want to cry.

I wanta cry because I'll miss

the light in her smile

That tells of her faith.

I wanta cry because I'll miss

the love from her life that sang out inside her.

I wanta cry because I'll miss

the Joy from her soul that set mine a-rocking.

Yes, she's gone, and I'll cry,

but not too long... not long,

because she didn't live her life

in tears, but in Song:

In songs of Hope, Praise, and Love.

She lived her life in song, and you can

        still hear her if you listen...

Listen...

   Listen to the Soul

   Listen to the Joy

   Listen to the Love

Listen to her sing, and you wouldn't need

          to cry, but you would.

She's gone,

But the Soul that she kneaded into her song,

and the love she gave the world is a part of us all.

Mahalia is gone and I want to cry...

But I don't think I will.

    I think...

        I think...

           I'll sing.

FOR UNCLE HOMER

You got a good man there, Lord:
   One who took the lesson of life
   and taught love and humility
   to all he touched.
   One whose gentleness grew
   from confidence and a
   Joy of life.
   One who knew the truth in "Brother"
   before he learned the meaning of self.
   You got a good man there, Lord:
   One who found love pliable,
   and stretched it from
   his heart to ours.
   One whose selfless love
   made him big enough to share
   and man enough to cry.
You got a good man there, Lord:
   You could tell by the way
   the children ran to him.
   Wait, you'll see,
   when the Children of Heaven
   flock to the Gate
   to take his gentle hand.

BERNSTEIN

The baton,

    The wand,

        The lightning rod,

            throbbing with power alive in the man;

Magic of songs

    travels his soul

        to

    The baton,

        The wand,

            The lightning rod,

    And emerges an echo of God.

That lightning wand,

    pointing and jabbing and slicing the air;

      Whole body rockin'

        and jumpin'

        and shaking the earth,

          A cathartic dance

            that shakes loose

          goose-bumps

        that sprout on my skin.

FOR SALLYE

First love
where are you and
why do you haunt me still?

I'm not fifteen anymore,
but forty. Does it
bother me that we never
made it, and that some
thing is unfinished inside me?

Unfinished?
It was hardly started.
I couldn't even look you
straight on, except from afar, or through
shy adolescence fingers, And

I never really touched
you, except at that school
dance one heavenly after afternoon...
And I never loved you
except in my dreams.

But I learned from you first
love. I learned new and
exciting feelings, like
how to care, how to need,
and how to conquer pain.

You were my seed of love
and I thank you still for
the flowers I can give.

Where are you first love?
I'd love to find you,
look you straight on and
place a rose in your hair.

SOUL SISTER

(For Marie Kelly)

I'm sure
we were friends
before we met,
and that some measure
of what I am comes from you.
On a distant star
our souls, each with a single virtue,
must've touched and drew, one from the other,
a quality not common before.
Your gift mingled with the essence of me
and created a new sensation to share.
I gave you tears,
      you gave me laughter.
I gave you peace,
      you gave me honesty.
I gave you courage,
      you gave me humility.

We touched,
and like electricity giving up sparks,
we grew in character until we
approached being born.
We hitched a ride home on the same comet,
but touched earth at separate times.

We knew nothing of our times before
until our paths crossed...
In the instant our eyes met,
our hearts exchanged another gift and
I knew I was your Brother.

MARY

Why do they come to you?
Why do they come
        haggard and wasted,
           crawling to you?
Come with drooping shoulders,
        dragging hearts,
           and tuneless songs,
             to you?

        Why?

Is it
   that in your presence
      they feel your warmth surfacing,
        and try to wrap themselves in it?
Or, do they hear in your voice
        the melody of hope,
          and dare to wish a tune for themselves?
Or, do they see in your eyes,
        the puppy of love
    desperately searching a home of its own... ?
      And dare to hope to capture him?

LOVE IS
REASON ENOUGH
(for Dave Cantral)

To see the world smile is reason enough
to give your smile to a stranger,
and to call him friend.

To feel the world breathe is reason enough
to blow bubbles with that bratty
kid down the block.

To hear the world giggle like a six-year-old
is reason enough to put on a nose
and make like a clown.

To feel the world's love is reason
enough to be yourself
and let the people experience
the beauty that is you.

Loving is reason enough.
It's easy... just love the
child within you and
let him come out.

GO AND PREACH THE WORD

(For Jai and Jerry on being ordained)

We have found you worthy,
Said the men of the Cloth...
And license you to preach the Word.

They said you can preach, now.
"So, now you a preacher man, huh?"
　　　Said the man of the street...
"Go ahead, bro, soothe folks
as you collect them fine clothes,
fine cars, and fine women. Yeah,
you got it made, baby...
you got the perfect scam...
　　　You can preach now."

They said you can preach, now.
　　"You can make us rock now..."
Said the members of the church.
　"You can preach soulfully, now.
　　Make us dance. Make us rock...
　Make us say, amen,
　　You got the right now.
They said you can preach, now."

"Live My Will",
Said the Lord of Hosts.
"This creature, man,
has said you can preach now...
But I placed the whisper in your heart
that blossomed into a calling.

Deliver messages that'll make'em
rock and say amen...
But make your life the sermon
I'll applaud".

KIM

who says she's no poet
is at least,
a love poem...
Crisp and compact like haiku,
she's the image of beauty and courage:
Risking all in a Sunday School recital,
she plants seeds of courage that sprout
into a new risk and new growth.

She wraps her fears in courage,
as she battles miscues, mistakes, and discords,
only to adding substance, lines and
stanzas to the poem she is.
Play.
Play on, Dear Girl...
I hear no discords. Your
fingers glide over the keys
and the sound that you share
is the poetry of your soul.
The beauty of her
growing into
something grand, stirs
my spirits more than
any spoken word. She
is poetry that lives
and brings new joy
stanza upon
          stanza.

BARBARA

Nothing but disbelief.

No tears, no pain.   Nothing.
How can you cry about a damn lie?
Barbara dead? Nonsense!
Nonsense.

Am I supposed to fall to the ground
weep like a real man to show how much
I loved her... loved what she was?

But,
I love you now, Barbara...
(Did I ever tell you that?)
You can't be gone.
You'll be back to work Monday
and we'll talk and laugh and   talk...

A part of my beauty
has been pushed just
beyond my reach. I
feel sad for me.

Damn it, Barbara...!
I had so much more to learn from you.

ART

I'm glad we didn't let
the moment pass. It would
have buried our friendship
among the noises of clanging
glasses and after-theater
chatter.

But we held the wings of the
fluttering moment long enough
for us to exchange our spirit
instead of smoke.

We accepted each for the one-
ness he is. Friends. With no
expectations, but with joy in
the other's triumph. No de-
mands, but with acceptance of
support from the other. Yet,
it is not the taking, or the
giving, that strengthens our
bond, but the frailties.

My failures bred in me
heart enough to reach down
to where I've been, to lift you
to a higher place... And likewise,
when I'm deep in the pit of myself,
with all my imperfections sticking
out like thorns,
you carefully reach down
through the spikes
and lift, not caring
about the pain.

(for Art Winslow)

TWO BY JEANETTE

TENANT

My love--   I'm inside you--
Feel that extra little beat
below your heart?
The warm glow in your
secret hiding places?

You let me in and
I took up residence.
You're sharing your body-house
with a tenant...   but
a conscientious tenant.
One who will take the best care
of your property and tread softly
on those places marked
"fragile."

WHEN WE'RE TOGETHER

He looks... as if expecting
    something great in me,
not knowing the only
  'great in me
    is when he's in me...

But he's here
  coloring my nonsense
    in bright shades
      of love

    changing my dark purple days
    to yellow and red

Making mountains out of
  the mole hill moments
    of my life!

IN LOVE AGAIN

AGAIN

I fell in love again last night.
This time
      with a young fertile mind
               called
                    Kathy.
She was as easy to talk to
      as my reflection on a mirror pond.
She was as warm as the summer sun
      and full of the color of its face
She was as lovely
      as the childlike innocence
          that strings
          My love
            from
          Heart
            to
          Heart.

ELEVATOR TRAGEDY

i think i like you.
the way you carry yourself
the way you look, the smile
i imagine.   i think
i like you...

how can i find out, how
                can i know?

risk a hurt,
   risk a blow!

            HI THERE, SWEET STUFF!

                omygod.

PERFECT GENTLEMAN

Yes,
coffee sounds nice,
thank you.

> *Mmm nice.*
> *Name tag spells denise,*
> *but that smile... delight.*
> *I bet she carries on her*
> *tray the hearts of a*
> *thousand tasteless men...*
> *plus mine.*

Thank you.
Yes, a couple a
minutes'll be fine.

> *Boy, look at that walk...*
> *whatabounce.*
> *Wonder if she'd...? naw!*
> *But there goes my heart,*
> *tumblin' from her tray and*
> *bouncin' to the rhythm of her walk.*
> *It's outta control now, rollin' wild*
> *all over the place.*
> *Maybe I can trap it under the table...*
> *ah, i got you! No. Oh, no...*
> *A dainty foot. Dear...*
> *you're standing on my heart, dear...*
> *but what a nice foot...*
> *what a nice leg...*
> *what a...*

What?! Yes!
Yes I am. A
number four breakfast.
Eggs over easy. Wheat toast.

>*Whew, what a number!*
>*walkin' away with my heart*
>>*stuck to her shoe like bubble gum.*
>*Here she comes again*
>*smiling that smile and walkin'*
>*all over my heart.*
>*Gotta do something.*
>*Gotta say something*
>*dashing and forward to recover my*
>*heart...*
>*something like:*
>*"Hey Baby, how'd you like*
>*an afternoon of maddening*
>*delight and...*

Eh...Yes, everything was fine...
A delight. Have to bring the
wife and kids next time.

>*Guess I leave that heart*
>*as a tip.*

IF YOU CATCH ME LOOKING

If you catch me looking at you,
it's because
you're so striking...
You strike a chord
that's tuned to my heart
and I love it.
It makes me move and
wanna be where you are...
It makes me wanna
touch you
and hold you and
whisper to your mind
that you're all right with me.
If you catch me looking at you...
Feel Good!

JOY

The space
where my heart was
is filled with tears
that flowed down my breast
and sank into my heart-
place as Joy.

ONE LINE

Plant you joy
among my tears and
watch it grow.

TURNING ME ON

Can the whole world see

I love you?

I'm trying to be discreet.

I think you cause a glow

in me

The whole damn world

can see.

THE ALMOST AFFAIR

There was

    the movement toward your hand

        that reached out to mine

with a healthy passion...

    But I halted a moment

        in what it meant,

And you passed my hesitation

    to another eager hand.

LISTEN TO THE GOOD THINGS

Can you stand all these good
                sounds about you?

Can you balance on the
                pedestal of new love?

Can you stand another heart
                beating at your breast?

Well listen up, baby
        'cause you make it happen
           in being who you are.

You're placed up there high,
        where you can really hear
           how neat you make me feel.

I WANT TO LISTEN

I wish I could woo you with
          a song of tomorrow.

But today, myself, and a poem
          is what I have to give.

Tomorrow belongs to you
          and your music...
             a Symphony.

          I want to listen!

LUST

Like the burning ash
       of a trashy novel,
my gluttony floats,
         burning hot,
and lights on the
    cold and
       hungry laps
     of my
      fantasies.

NIGHT FANTASY

You came to me
a crier of promise.
Telling me you've
seen my soul
decked out loud
like high in
fidelity among the
the embracing
rose trees.
And that you would come for me
under a rose scented cloud of delight.
    I lied, with hungry eyes:
            No way...
      for I am true and never...
        and never...
          and never...
  I woke up
    groping for you.

ONLY THE EYES

My love grew
three times between itself
and the beckoning in your
eyes whispering
        Hello.

Today,
and in joys to come,
my wild eyes flash
fiercely to the rhythm:
    "Hold me! Love me! Hold me..."
          as the soft light in your
eager eyes utter...
    "Touch me!"

And when our eager
        carnal bliss
          is wrapped in the soft
        patch-quilt of aged delights,
and exchanged for the lesser...
          yet more exquisite,
    Touch of mind,
I will still reach out from
        my grayed brow
      and draw you close...
    to warm and be warmed
      by the Love in our eyes.

SUPERKIDS

DONOL'S HAPPY

Donol
named his carpet "Happy"
'cause he has to smile
to make
it go.

He
smiles easy
and cruises
smoothly from
garden to garden
and plants sun-
flowers as parting
gifts... or
Donol laughs
and makes Happy
zip and dip and
loop 'd loop
through the
soft cloudy
hoops of
heaven...

APRIL

You are like the slow
unwrapping of a beautiful
and precious gift. Each
day reveals a new facet
of the beauty to come.

You are
my little whiz-kid,
music maker and foot
racer.

You are built for speed,
climbing dreams and
echoing the sounds of heaven.

Work hard
on the foot races...
bring home medals around your neck
and place them high upon your wall...
Let 'em shout: "Winner," that you are.

And in times of triumph,
when crowds gather 'round like subjects,
and the glory sort-a floats you
like a dream... remember:

You're not a strider,
but a striver, climbing clouds,
making music, and finding
the glory in your soul, and
the joy in your giving.

KRISS' GIGGLE

Kriss,
Your giggle
is a laughing
magical wine.

One sip and I'm
a little boy
rockin' my head
to the rhythm of
your silly walk
and outrageous
talk.

I laugh 'til the
tears run down
my cheeks and
flow into my
mouth as mellow
lemon wine.

I spin on the floor
like a merry-go-
round and twirl
and grow like whipped
cream 'til I am your
tall and lanky,
giggly twin.

SUPERKID, CYNDI

I love it
that you can cry
at a bird's broken wing, or
at a heart out of tune
               with love.

I love it
that you can feel for
the butterfly, the Juniper and Me...

I love it that you can
spend your warmth making
me care too.

I love it
that you can still laugh
with your Dad and
make him glad to be with you...
To see, in you eyes,
the Joy of his life.

I love it
that you can smile and
awaken the world
to the beauty of
your simple love.

I love you, Cindi,
and want to be
more like
You.

MONICA
ORANGE SHERBET AND
HOT CHOCOLATE

That's you in orange, Baby;
Hot, sweet and sassy.
I should never
reveal this, but
When you
wanna con
something
from your
Daddy, Dear...
you stand
a better chance
if you wear orange,
'Cause
in orange
you are such a
delight...
Your cheeks
light up,
your eyes
twinkle, and
the glow from
your soul
melts my
nonchalance.

SUNDAY SUNDAY

(Kriss at eight years old)

Krissie's eyes,
    (like caged
        curiosity)
darted in
    and out,
    and all around
    the windy
        sermon...

And somewheres
        'tween Jonah
        swallowing
        a whale,
    and the Pharisees
    kissing
        Judas...
She marveled,
    as her feet
      took flight,
    and
    danced
      on the ceiling.

I'M BUSY
(for Mari)

Little girl,
daughter of mine,
don't pester me now.   Now
who said you could climb on
my knee?   And that's my chest
you're pounding on. Watch it,
Pumpkin, you almost poked me
in the eye. Hey, hey, get
your finger out of my mouth...
you're tickling my soul and I'm
too busy to play.
                    So, little one,
stop poundin' and pokin'
and ticklin'... Just let
me be.   Go...
Go tickle your Mama...
                         Yeah...
She sittin' over there
smiling and lookin' good...
Go sit on her knee and
hit on her.
                    Ah... Wait!
Wait a minute, Pumpkin...
Why don't you stay over here and play,
and I'll go over there and
hit on your lovely Mama.

   Hello little mama...
         Wanna play?

IF YOU TOOK SUE

This friend of my daughter,
who has become another
daughter, is very special:

If you took her essence,
rolled it into a big purple
ball and tossed it down the
alley of life, you'd score
a strike every time.

If you took her goodness
you could be a magician and
reverse frowns, make hurts
vanish and fill empty hearts
with joy.

If you took her understanding
you could be the perfect friend;
knowing when to hold out your
hand and when to hold your tongue.

If you took her laugh,
you could be a musician
and lead the world in the
music of laughter.

And if you took her smile,
you would have a connection
with the stars... because they
surely smiled the day
She was born.

CECE

That gal
sure can jump, sure
can run, sure
can put that shot.

She's
got the gift. She's
got the gift. She's got
the gift of
flight.

Sure
can jump, sure
can run, sure can
put that shot, Sure
can smile!

Gal, you
got more power
in that dimpled smile
than in all your runnin'
and all your jumpin',
and all your winnin',
could muster in a
lifetime, 'cause
your smile touches
the winner in
us all.

Sure
can jump, sure
can run, sure can
put that shot, Sure
can smile!

MARK

You're
a charmer on skates,
whizzing through life
on genius and con.

You put on your skates
and glide, feather light,
over unbroken eggs and
similar hearts. You
kiss the girls, and
whirl away to the
Summer sounds.

You're beautiful, Man.

You "put on" your smile and
you can con the game from
Flim-Flam himself.
You spread it on so warm
you can charm the yoke
outta an egg and not
crack it's shell.

You're cool, Man.

You're all right, Man.
    You're beautiful...
        You're cool...

But in the games of youth,
take care you don't scramble
the eggs you intend to hatch, or
break the heart you'll
need for love.

GETTING TOGETHER WITH MYSELF

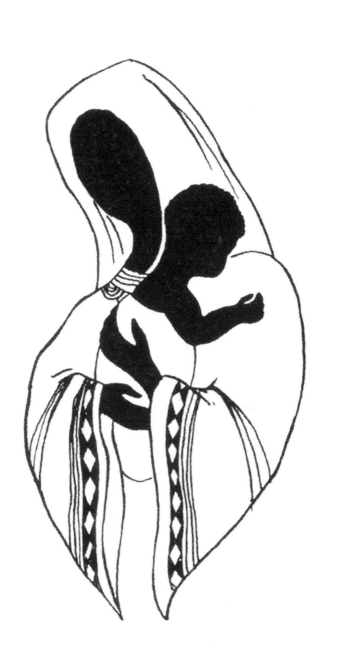

BLACK LOVE

Black
was a hurting word
until I looked deep
into my mother's face.
She was Black as her
Bible and beautiful as
its verse: Black as
polished ebony and
beautiful as freedom;
Black as Africa and
beautiful as
heritage. Black
as me, and
beautiful as
Love.

GETTING TOGETHER
WITH MYSELF

I must wring out my surface Blackness

until it drips ebony pools at my feet.

Then

my colorless soul

must get itself

together,

and sop

that

B

l

a

c

k

n

e

s

s

UP!

UNMASKED

"We wear the mask that grins and lies......"
(Paul Lawrence Dunbar)

We no longer wear the mask.

The heat of our emergence
from the tangled lies of history
has tempered our Souls and
consumed our false faces.

We no longer wear the mask.

Black before you is the real me...
    Not grinning
      Not lying,
        But true...

True to myself,
    who bears some scars from
      removing the mask...

True to my Fathers
    who wore the mask so I
      might endure...

True to my Children
    who will wear no mask
      and bear no scars.

We no longer wear the mask.

So scrape the mask from your
mind, and let's come honestly,
        face to face...
fulfilling the Dream
    of our children in peace.

THOUGHTS OF A STOLEN ONE

Africa,
  Africa,
    Oh sweet Africa...
      you are forever me.
You are the land of my mother,
    the land of my blood,
      the land of my soul.

Are you still there sweet Africa?
            Still there?

But how can you be,
    without my hands to make you real?
      How can I still be?

How can I still be
      without your warm earth
            beneath my feet?

Oh, Africa,
    you are only a thought away and
          the hope of my broken life.

Yesterday I looked into a pond and forgot.
  I saw Africa and freedom in my eyes.

        Oh please...
  Please steal me back.
    Please hold me once again to
        your dark bosom and
        let my tears
          help your flowers grow.

TODAY'S BLACK MAN

Today's Black man
has the strength of character
that gives beauty to his Blackness
and content to his dreams.

Today's Black Man...
Is the might...
the Dream-Power... the source...
behind the Woman who shares
his creating.

He is Father to today's rude child
who will walk tall and straight
in the peace of tomorrow.

His love is the power
behind the dreams of
his children that will set them free.

Today's Black Man...
is father to all Blacck children,
teaching them worth
through honest example.

DREAMS AND WISHES

DREAMS

Untried dreams
are just snow
flakes in the
heat of life.

BUT WHO?

I knew somebody

else

had the world

by the tail,

'Cause

when I grabbed for it,

there wasn't nothing

there

but air...

THE GRAND CREMATION

Let the wild dogs

devour me

and spread me

Miles

Across

The

Plains.

DUTY

Gotta go

Gotta go.

Got ta go!

Can't go,

Gotta

go

to

Work!

LAST MONDAY'S DIET

Last Monday's diet
　　suffered defeat,
　　　when I passed all those signs
　　　　shoutin' nothin' but eat.
Neons winkoning' and beckonin'
　　and beggin' to raise
　　　that innocent desire
　　　　deprived.

Just a tauntin' and a teasin'
　　and a gettin' on down
　　　with "waistliner Specials"
that somehow arrive
　　as Lumberjack Combos
　　　with inch-thick fillets,
　　and Royal made sundaes
　　　that I've craved for days.
And it all piles on
　　as calories to burn
　　　in the diet that starts...
　　Next
　　　Monday.

UNREAL

A smile with a purpose,

    Like hollow bananas

       and empty piñatas,

Has only the surface.

FOR REAL

It has to be real
as funny-face pancakes,
cool mud oozing 'tween toes,
or green-peach stomach aches.

It has to be catchy
like measles, happy
like monkeys, and
warm like sunbeams

It has to be free
as rain and fresh
as a first kiss.

To be real,
a Smile has to
tickle from the toes, and
twinkle in the eyes.

LOST THOUGHT

Yesterday

I had a thought about you.

I should have written it down

                    because it

said in poetry...

            in few words,

    just how lovely you are, and

        how warm you make me feel.

The thought was just right...

            I

        wish

            I

            had

                it

                right

                now.

FILTERED SYMPHONY

or

Beginning Band Concert

Proud parents
with filters
for ears,
and
dreams
for vision,
sit at
attention
and
witness
themselves
make
flawless
music
with the
New York
Philharmonic.

THIRD GRADE RAIN

*(The following is the result of a visit
to several third grade classes at
Spaulding Elementary School, Pomona, Ca.)*

On a rainy Tuesday morning
they said they couldn't write.

"We only third graders
and not that kinda
bright... 'sides, poetry
is sissy stuff, not for
big kids like us."

"My dear third graders,
just now you made a poem.
You smiled at me, you said hello...
You made me warm inside

Now, poetry's not just
words lifeless on a page, but
something live inside us...
like the glow from being loved;
or like the smile we bury deep...
when we think we'd rather sulk...
but that daddies can somehow
hook and tease on out of us.

So,
If you can dream
          (for anything)
If you can lend a hand
          and feel real good;
If you can belly laugh
          or bellyache;
If you get wet in the rain
          or warmed in the sun;
If you love spinach,
          or hate asparagus;
If you can breathe,
          or touch
    or love,
     you have already
      made a poem.

So, they took that rainy Tuesday
and put them poems on down.

> *I like the rain,*
> *   It's fun.*
> *I like the rain,*
> *   It's beautiful.*

> *I love the rain...*
> *I run outside*
> *Open my mouth wide*
> *And drink as much rain as*
> *I can!*

I watched the rain come down
my windows. It looked like
soldiers fighting in the water.

The rain makes me wet and soggy
            like wet cornflakes.
            I don't like the rain.

Rain
It's cold and
wet, and it
comes and comes
from Clouds.

The rain makes the road slick
                    and me sick.

I let me dog and cat inside
while it rained cats and
dogs outside.

While in the rain
            I saw a frog.
It was a big ole bullfrog...
I already had fishes in
        my fish tank and
            couldn't keep him.

The weather was
        raining cold chills...
It was so cold
        I couldn't go.

MY YOUTH'S NOT SPENT

My youth's not spent,
it's in my heart like
a gift.

Each morning
I untie my heartstrings,
place that precious
twinkle of youth in my
eyes, and challenge
the day as a spendthrift.

I celebrate today
for what I'll do tomorrow.
And I don't dwell
on the days I've spent,
but on the gift of today
alone.

Everyday, now,
I carry to the lake,
an empty canvas,
an assortment of
brushes and paints, and
my seventy-nine years of
mistakes and delights.

I sit,
a sponge soaking in
the truant teenagers
necking under the elm tree;
the silent cat stalking
a playful bluejay;
and the old-timer jogging
his two miles a day.

> With my brush, I
> seek to capture the
> thing that makes a
> child a child, a
> man a man, and love
> love.

> I touch color upon
> color and approach
> the particulars that
> make God God.

So,
if I never untie another bow,
or hear another child laugh, and
if I never stroke another canvas,
don't mourn too much for me, 'cause
I will have spent my life to the moment,
and would dutifully pass my brush
to the runner at the lake.

ALSO BY RICHARD D. GORDON

Orange Sherbet And Hot Chocolate (Poetry)
The Bulldog and The Bear (a play)
Othello in Hell (a play)
Evergreen (a play)
The Calling of Richard Allen
  (A story poem on the founder of the African
Methodist Episcopal Church)

R. D. Gordon has also had poetry published in
Essence Magazine, and is featured in Lindsay
Patterson's anthology: A Rock Against The
Wind.

Richard Gordon, pictured here for the first edition, with his son Donol, received his B.A. in Theater Arts, from California State University, Fullerton. He considers himself more an actor-playwright than a poet. Orange Sherbet and Hot Chocolate is his first book of poetry.

Richard Gordon, pictured here with his son Donol (Richard D. Gordon, Jr.), for the second edition   Since the first edition of Orange Sherbet, Richard Gordon has been writing poetry and drama, and teaching . . . including twelve years at Cal-State University at Fullerton.